RACE

RACE

Reducing **A**frican-American **C**rime
Effectively

By
Vernolda L. Dilworth

To order additional copies of this book, contact:
Xlibris Corporation
1-888-795-4274
www.Xlibris.com
Orders@Xlibris.com
99079

Contents

This book is dedicated to my most-admired
hero and role model, my mother,

Momie M. Dilworth

"She is my Queen"

Preface

I have a great love for teenagers. No I'm not crazy! I just understand that their lives are challenging and very difficult. In spite of what everybody else think . . . I know that the teenage years are the most difficult times in ones life. Most adults seem to have forgotten those days and think that teenagers are just causing problems and turning everybody else's world upside down for the fun of it? But I believe that the teenage years are the most vital-real world . . . hands on—training . . . one will receive before they enter into their adult life. And we must be there to support and encourage them along the way.

As a middle age woman who has spent over twenty—five years working and interacting with both delinquent males and females, and being a single mother of a well adjusted wonderful 25-year-old son. I can speak from a personal and professional experience with great knowledge and compassion. I am on a mission to motivate our young men and women. I am mostly focusing on my young black brothers in this book, because I have such a passion to see the young black man get excited about living a successful productive life. And without a doubt, our men will be the ones that will make the quickest most effective impact on our society. That's right! Believe it brothers. You are the key to this problem. You were made and created to be the head of the household. And our society will not see lasting results until you take your place in your position as the authoritarian and leader of the family.

Let me go ahead and apologize and warn you in advance so you can brace yourself, this book is raw, uncut, uncensored, and straightforward. I'm sure it will be offensive to some people. But I must talk candid and lay it all out on the line to get your attention and make you think and want to change. We will discuss some of the major factors that influence our young black generation. I will provide a fresh simple way to empower young people to make life changing positive choices that will help them to reach their greatest potential and never make another bad decision in their life. We are all of the human race and we must live our lives in a way that we can be proud that we have ran our course and fulfilled our destiny and purpose. There is nothing more satisfying in life than to be able to pass on your legacy to the next generation knowing that you have done your best in this race called life.

Chapter One

Let's Race

The color of my skin no longer hinders me. I can go anywhere and do anything with no regard to the color of my skin. Or, should I say, I can go anywhere and do anything without blatant discrimination and racism. Discrimination and racism still exist today . . . but it must be disguised in some type of hidden agenda. You and I both know that the black race still has not yet overcome, but we do demand that discrimination and racism be disguised or kept under cover. Millions of dollars have been paid out to black people due to discrimination lawsuits. Times have changed and white people are now being held accountable for their actions. I'll be the first to admit that discrimination is still alive. But in today's society discrimination is like having your cell phone on vibrate mode. It is still ringing . . . but it must not ring out loud or out in the open, where it can be heard or recognized or someone will have to pay. You know what I mean? Blacks now have equal rights and opportunities as all other Americans. The law of the land protects us today from being treated as second class . . . less than human citizens. So I can boldly say with confidence and assurance that I can go anywhere and do anything with no regard to the color of my skin, and so can you.

Not too long ago, white people could treat black people in any way they wanted to . . . and they did not have to justify their actions or answer to anyone. And there was no recourse, help, or protection for us. All the black man could do was take it. And a lot of times it would cost them their lives. Thank God! Times have changed and whites are now held accountable in the twentieth century. I know what you are thinking . . . that is in the past and it has nothing to do with me today. I was born in an integrated society, and I have been interacting with white people all my life. You can probably even say that you have some white friends who are closer to you than most blacks. And that is all good and that is the way it should be . . . but I want you to understand that it has not always been this way. Our ancestors had to go through a lot to make sure that you could enjoy all these wonderful protections and privileges that you have today.

Now I need you to explain something to me. With all these privileges and protections in place today, why are blacks still at the bottom? Why do we have 80 percent of blacks in our prisons? Why are our young people not motivated to go to school, work, and take care of themselves and their families? I know these are some real hard questions . . . But what happened to being black, proud, and free? Be honest and look around. We have more freedom and privileges today more than ever before . . . but we as a black race are in the worse shape culturally today than we were seventy-five years ago. If you don't agree with me that our black race seems to be deteriorating every single day, you should stop reading this book now because we are not living in the same world. The black man is refusing to take on the responsibility for his family by making sure that his kids and wife are loved, taken care of, and safe. A man should make sure that all of his family's basic needs are met: food, shelter, and clothing.

Blacks are living like they are in slavery today more than ever before. Generations of families have been satisfied with waiting on the government slavery welfare handouts. Our men are absent from the family. The women either refuse to work or they work night and day to support the family while the children are running wild and raising themselves. The welfare system is overburdened. Many families use the welfare system by getting everything they can for free (food stamps, SSI, welfare). Then on the side they try and supplement the little free government monies by hustling men, churches, and the streets usually by selling drugs or doing something illegally under the cover. These types of lifestyles are not producing lasting prosperous results. We are just living . . . barely staying afloat.

This mediocre way of living just keeps us in the same old rut generation after generation without accomplishing anything worthwhile. No houses, no land, no inheritance to leave for the next generation. The only thing we leave is a poor example and lots of poverty and despair. Any way you look at it, we are still right back to my original question: Why are blacks still at the bottom? With all the rights and privileges we have today what has gone wrong? Things are not adding up. We are no longer bound by slavery . . . "We are free." We do not have to live on the plantation and work night and day in the fields. We are no longer bought and sold into slavery and separated from our families. But we have more of our black men in prison than any other race. What has happened? Have our young black men decided that they do not want to be free, and have decided to return to the modern day slavery—"prison?" I know you are saying, "I can't believe that she said that." I must admit it is very difficult for me to be so candid and put myself out there like this, but I must lay all the facts out on the table and keep it real so I can get your attention. It appears to me that the black man has given up and taken himself out of the human race. I know, not all of our black men are locked up, but trust me, we have too many wasting away in prison. I must commend my brothers who are keeping their freedom and living a productive, successful free life. Thank you for doing the right thing to keep your freedom. Thank you for being an example and proof that it can be done. We need more good examples like you, and *this* is the purpose of this book. So keep your head up and let the world know that you have it together and do whatever you can to pull another brother up.

It is time for our black men to get up and take advantage of all of the rights and privileges we have today and get back into the human race. Our nation need our black men to take their places in the family and in the society to ensure that our black male population does not become extinct. You heard me right! *Extinct.* Successful black men are so few that today's society has placed the black man on the extinction list. Which means at the rate things are going our black males will cease to exist . . . no longer living . . . zero . . . no more . . . gone! And you can't blame the white man. We are destroying ourselves by refusing to work, selling drugs, gang banging, stealing, and killing each other. Believe me when I say, the white man want to see you doing better. They are tired of spending the taxpayer's dollars to build larger prisons to take care of you because you refuse to obey the law and take care of yourself. I know this is hard to accept, but the truth must be told. So you can't use the excuse, "I'm black and the white man keep doing this to me to keep me down." The law of the land protects us today from being treated as second-class citizens; so what is your excuse now? So you must agree with me regardless of what situation you find yourself in today, it is your choice and your actions that have put you there. So don't blame anyone, but yourself. You are your own person and no one can control you, but you. So take advantage of the rights and privileges you have today. Blacks now have equal rights and opportunities as all other Americans. So you must decide whether you want to do better and get back into the human race. I am challenging you to join the race toward living your best life, no matter what your age or circumstances are today. If you choose to take this challenge, I promise you that you will discover that you have potential that you have not tapped into or used. And your best life is yet to come. You are free and protected to go anywhere and do anything your heart desires. So let's get down to the nitty-gritty and race.

Chapter Two

On Your Mark

You have accepted my challenge, and you are now ready to get into this race. Let me explain the rules of this race so you can get on the mark. First of all, you are running in the human relay race for life. This is the most important thing you will ever do in your life. Your whole purpose and existence for living is to run in this race. The next generation is depending on us to maintain and preserve life so that they can have a fair chance at living the great dream. You are designated to run in the last and final leg of this race. You have an advantage . . . because the first two legs of the race were ran by some very amazing people. They believed in giving life all they had. Quitting or dropping out of the race and giving up because things got hard were never options for them . . . and you should have that same attitude. They were willing to, and did, die in order to remain in this race and make things better for the people who would come after them. So you and I are both still reaping the benefits of their hard work. In order to understand how important you are in this race, you must understand what has happened in the first two legs of the race before you.

The first leg of the race was ran by our sisters and brothers from Africa. In the early eighteenth century, hundreds of thousands of black men, women, and children were captured, chained, beaten, and branded like cattle. Then they were put into the hole of a sailing ship and carried across the Atlantic. Upon arrival in the United States, they were sold into slavery and separated from their families. Let me make sure you get a good picture and understand what really happened to them. First of all, they were torn away from their families never to see or hear from them again. Can you imagine never being able to see or hear from your family again? You do not know if they are dead or alive. I want you to think about this situation for a moment. Imagine that from this point on, you will never be able to see your brother, sister, son, daughter, father, or mother ever again. There is no way for you to contact them and you don't know if they are dead or alive. There are no letters, no e-mails, no text messages, or phone calls . . . no way to make contact whatsoever. You can't even contact a friend, who may be able to tell you how they are doing. And from this point on you never hear from or see them ever again in life. That is what I call having a broken heart and having something to worry about. This is what our ancestors had to deal with on a daily basis. But they never gave up.

Now tell me what are your problems? When was the last time you were made to work in the fields and brutally whipped if you wanted to stop and get a drink of water? How did it feel when the "masta" took a metal rod and heated the rod over an open fire flame and stuck it to your arms and legs and branded you like a cow? Oh yeah, this did happen! If you are like me, you are thinking, I'm so glad that I did not have to go through that . . . but I don't want you to forget that someone had to endure that kind of inhuman treatment in order for you to be where you are at today. God knew you and I could not have endured that part of the race . . . so he gave us something that we can do. He knew that we can obey the law, keep our freedom, get an education, work, and take care of our families.

In the first leg of the race, blacks were killed, burned, and lynched at anytime by the white man with no punishment for their actions. All the black man could do was take whatever the "masta" wanted to do to them. I am so glad that we are running in the last leg of this race, because we clearly could not have done the job that they had done in the first part of the race. They did an excellent job . . . and they have finished their course. A lot of the times it meant they had to give up their lives, which they did willingly to make it better for you and I today. They have finished their course and accomplished what they had to do . . . that important part of the race is completed and you and I cannot go and rerun that part for them, and neither can they come back and finish our part for us.

In 1863, President Lincoln signed the Emancipation of Proclamation, which allowed blacks the right to fight in the civil war. This helped in moving the black race toward gaining freedom and reconstruction had begun. I'm going to call this our second leg of the race. The Civil Rights Bills of 1874 gave African Americans freedom of movement throughout the states. Blacks were allowed to move in public places such as stores, restaurants, bus stations, and railroads without distinction because of their race or previous condition of servitude. But we still had to sit on the back of the bus. Enter through the back door of stores and restaurants. Use only those water fountains and toilets that were labeled as "colored." It was the beginning of blacks having equal protection. A lot of progress was made during this period, but we still had a lot of adversity to overcome. But again we had some special people to rise up to the occasion and take on the challenges of that day and time and finish their part of the race. Our ancestors have done their part and now it is up to you and I. The only way that we can show our forefathers that we admire and appreciate everything that they have done is by doing our best in everything that we do to take advantage of what they have made available for us.

Now that you understand what has happened before your leg in this race, you have to get excited about getting on the mark and being proud to carry this last leg and finish the human relay race. Believe me, when I say that your participation in this race is just as important as the ones that have ran before you. They cannot finish your part and you cannot redo their part. They are counting on us to finish this race. We are all equally important in this race and if you do not get on your mark and run this race all of their suffering will have been done in vain. We must step up and finish what they have started. Get on your mark, take your place in the right racing lane, and learn to take pride in where you come from. When you understand your history it will help you get directions on where you want to go.

After I learned what my ancestors had to endure to give me a better life, it motivated me to work through my little problems that I'm faced with today. I gained pride, purpose, and respect for myself. I wanted to be a part of this amazing human relay race. I wanted to count. I gained purpose knowing that I was needed to make this world a better place. When you understand that if you don't do your part, nothing that was done before you will matter. I am dedicated and willing to do my best to make them as proud of me as I am of them. Don't leave it up to somebody else to stand in the gap and make a difference. We need you . . . so make sure that you are doing your part. You are a key runner in this race. We need you . . . I need you. I know you are on the mark with me . . . right? It is time for us to get serious about our future and take advantage of what our ancestors have made available to us.

Chapter Three

Get Ready

Are you still here? That's great! I like that . . . It shows that you are serious about taking this challenge and getting back into the human relay race of life. This is the best decision that you have ever made. Things are getting better already because you are headed in the right direction. You are now on your mark and you realize that our ancestors are depending on you and I to finish what they have started. Now, let's get ready! In order to get ready, you must change your way of thinking. You are going to have to imagine yourself being successful. You must have a picture of what your end results should look like. This will help you stay focus and help you know what you are trying to accomplish. Getting ready starts in your mind. In order to get ready, you have to change your thinking and you must stop thinking about all your failures and disappointments. You must remember that change is not change until you change. And if you continue to do the same old things, you will continue to get the same old negative results. Have you ever heard the sayings, "what goes around comes around" and "you reap what you sow?" That is exactly what I'm trying to tell you about your negative thinking and actions. If you want to change and get some better results, you are going to have to be willing to do some new different things, so you can get some new different positive results. In order to get ready for this race you must be ready in your mind. Whatever you think about all the time will guide your actions and behavior. This is why it is so important for you to get your thinking corrected and have a positive attitude.

When you are ready in your mind, you will be willing to turn away from everything that will hinder you from reaching your goals. This is the hard part. You will have to give up all illegal criminal activity and thinking. You may have to stay away from friends and family members who are not willing to think and live right. If they do not want what you want or if they are not helping you reach your goals, it is okay to let them go. My mother always said, "Birds of the same feather will flock together." I did not understand what she was saying until I was grown. Basically, you surround yourself with people that are into the same things as you are. If they are not after the same things that you are after . . . let them go! Find yourself some friends who have a like-mind and the same goals as you have. When you are ready you will have your mind-set on doing the right things and your actions will follow your mind. So many people make the mistake of wanting to change their negative behavior, but they still have the same old negative thinking patterns. This will not work . . . you will not change your behavior until you change your way of thinking. It's impossible to change bad behavior without an attitude adjustment, which means you must change your way of thinking. Attitude is more important than facts. It is more important than your past, than education, than money, than circumstances, than failures, than successes, than what other people think, say, or do. Attitude is more important than appearance, giftedness, or skills. Your attitude will make or break you. The most remarkable thing is that we have a choice to make every day regarding the attitude we will embrace that day. We cannot change our past . . . we cannot change the fact that people will act in a certain way. We cannot change the inevitable. The only thing we can do is change the one thing we have, and that is our attitude. I am convinced that life is 10 percent of what happens to you and 90 percent of how you react. You are not responsible for everything that happens to you, but you are responsible for how you react to what does happen to you. So from this point on, do not ever give complete control of your attitude—the only thing that you have—to someone else. Be in charge of your own attitude. It is under your full control. It's really all you have.

Make sure you have a good attitude and you are setting positive goals. Get a good picture in your mind of what you want out of life. Your picture of success isn't the same as anyone else's, because you are a different and a unique individual. So you must first know who you are and what you want out of life. See yourself being successful in your mind and know what the picture is suppose to look like. Then stay focused, so come hell or high water you will keep working toward your success picture. If you are willing to think good wholesome law-abiding thoughts, your behavior and your actions will follow your thoughts. I guarantee you that you will see changes in your life. And so will other people. Everything starts in your mind and thinking first. So dream big and dream often. With every chance you get, imagine yourself living the good life. It is okay to daydream. Spend as much time as you can seeing yourself being successful. You cannot move forward until you change your way of thinking. Get your mind ready first and your behavior and actions will line up with your thinking and expectations. "Live out of your imagination, not your history."

Chapter Four

Go

Go! Once you take off, you can't look back or give up. You can't be concerned about what the other runners are doing all around you. This is an individual race. You must stay focused on your race and what you want out of life. It is up to you to make a life for yourself. You are at a point in your life when you must start to think about yourself as an individual. It doesn't matter what your family has done or what they should have done, but didn't. They cannot live your life for you and you cannot live their lives for them. We are talking about you. You came into this world as an individual with your own body and mind, and guess what? You are going to leave this world by yourself. So it is up to you to take responsibility for yourself. You can only control you. So right now I want you to get over what your parents and family have or have not done. I agree with you, yes, they have done you wrong. You have been abused, misused, and rejected like no one can imagine. But you are still here . . . and because you are still here you can change. So let all that hurt and frustration go and move on. You cannot go back and undo anything. It has happened. It is in your past and you can't change that. So stop reliving those bad memories in your mind over and over again. Remember you are now a positive thinker, and you have taken control of your attitude. So don't keep letting those negative things keep you from doing what you want to do today. "Let It Go" and "Move On." You have to take responsibility for yourself. You have to move forward and not look back or stop for anything or anyone. You are your own person. No one else can feel what you are feeling. Nor will they be held accountable for what you do. You must take responsibility and be willing to be held accountable for yourself. So stop blaming everybody else for your problems and failures. And get started on your way to your successful good life.

You have got to make up your mind to get started on changing your life. I know you have got excuses on why this will not work for you. We all do. But you are not so messed up that you can't change. Let me go ahead and get this straight right now. I agree with you . . . your parents are messed up . . . Yes, parents, I said it. "You are messed up!" Because if you had done the right things, your children will not be in the shape that they are in today. This book is not written for your parents. Because they have already messed up their lives and I'm trying to stop them from messing up your life too. Your parents are a big part of the reason why you are having so many problems now. But there is help for you. You have a long life in front of you. You must take control and stop this negative generational cycle now! Being a good parent is the most important job that was given to man to do. And when the parents stop parenting it causes a whole generation to start to deteriorate. Parenting is an important job and your parents have failed. But you will be a parent one day soon, if not already. And you must do the right things in order for your children to be successful and well adjusted. You must train a child and show them how to live. There is no other way! I know you have had to deal with parents who were not dependable, trustworthy, or honest. Your daddy was never around and you may not even know who he is. Or if he was around he did not invest any time or energy into your life. Your mother was so caught up into trying to find someone to love her and help support her, that she have had so many inappropriate sexual relationships in front of you that you don't know what real love feels like. You have been so hurt and frustrated about having to watch and not be able to do anything about your parents using and abusing drugs and alcohol. The bottom line is that they did not provide you with the safety, security, shelter, or love that you needed, but you are still here. And that says a lot. That means that you are a strong individual. You are just what is needed and is perfect for this last leg of this race. God has kept you here for a reason. You have survived and he has a plan for your life. So you've got to take your place and make up your mind to get started where you are at today. You must dig your heels in and not look back, quit, or give up on this race. Let the past be the past. You can be successful in spite of all the things you have had to endure as a child. You are not the only person who has been abused and misused physically, sexually, and emotionally. Yes, it hurts and it is hard to get over it, but you can't continue to be angry at the world. When you are angry, you are on a mission to make everybody feel as angry and hurt as you are. This is not the answer to your anger problem. Listen to me . . . the best way you can get back at the persons who have done you wrong is to show them that you are going to be somebody and rise above the things that have hurt you so bad. As long as you are acting out and fighting with the world because you are angry, they are in control of you. They have defeated you and you are just where they want you to be (a loser, a puppet on a string). You must have the attitude. "In spite of what someone did to me, I am going to do something with my life and be somebody." I am going to start today, right now. By doing this you take all the power away from them. Remember you are in control of you and no one else. You have to let it go and move on. Get over your past! Remember you are responsible for your own actions and you cannot control anyone but yourself. You can no longer use your childhood problems as an excuse to drop out of this race. You must be willing to forgive them and let go of all bitterness and hurt. Your parents have chosen a life for them, and you must choose a life for you. You are an individual and you can rise above all these negative circumstances, or you can continue in this same negative unproductive rut. Now if you were raised by good God-fearing parents who did all the right things, but you have rebelled and went against everything they have taught you at home and church, you just need to get up, shake it off, and get back on the right track. You know the right way. Just do it!

If you are willing to start making some changes, you are now off and running in the right direction. Take it slow! Move at your own pace. Stay focused and don't quit or look back. This race is not about who can run the fastest, but about who will endure to the end. And remember this is a life-long journey. You will soon find out that doing the right thing is not that easy. But you can do it! If you fall or stumble, get up and take off again. You can start over and over as many times as you need too. Just don't ever stop getting back up. No matter what happens, don't stop! You must keep pressing toward your finish line. Giving up in this race will cost you everything. And that is not an option. Once you get started, it is normal for you to experience some setbacks and problems, but you must keep getting up and starting over again!

Chapter Five

Run, Run, Run

You are now running, you have decided that what you are doing is not working for you. So now you are dedicated to doing your best to make some changes so you can have a better life. It is very important that you start to make some good decisions. If you continue to do what you have always done, you will continue to get what you have always got. If you keep doing the same old things over and over again, but you are looking for some different results, you are considered to be insane. And I know you are not insane or crazy because you are still reading this book. So now you know that if you want things to get better, you must be willing to make good decisions. If you want different results, you must do different things.

By now I hope you realize that you can choose your own destiny. The place you are at today came about by the decisions you have made in the past. All your failures and successes are a result of the decisions you have made in your life. Everything happens by the decisions you have made whether they are good or bad. You have created your life by your choices. It is so important that you make good decisions. I know you are saying, "I can't look into the future, so I don't know what to do. My decisions seem to be right and good at the time I am making them, but then later, I find myself in trouble because I've made a bad decision." I'm going to help you learn how you can never make another bad decision in your life. Or if you do make a poor decision, you will know it before you do it. One thing you must do to make a good decision is to think about the end results first, both the positive and negative consequences before you act or react to anything. Every action or reaction have consequences. There is no way around this principle. Some consequences are good and some are bad. You have to look at them all and make a choice. For example, let's look at a very common decision that you must make every day.

Decision: Should I skip school or work today?

Remember that there are always consequences both good and bad. You have to be willing to accept and want *good results* and *consequences* . . . this is your key to a good successful life.

Decision: Should I skip school or work today?

Good consequences/results for skipping school or work:
I will get to do what I want to do that day.
Have fun and relax.

Bad consequences/results for skipping school or work:
Have to lie to my parents, boss, and teachers.
Miss all my classes.
Get behind in all my schoolwork.
Lower my grades/GPA.

Put more work on my coworkers.
Have to hide and lie so I will not get caught.
Lose the respect of my employer.
Lose pay . . . get fired.

I'm sure that you can think of some more consequences both good and bad, but I hope that you can clearly see that the bad negative consequences are a lot more and not worth skipping school or work. So a person who is wanting to live a good productive successful life would choose to go to school and or work because the consequences of skipping school or work is not worth a little temporary satisfaction of having fun all day and not being held accountable. Overall, it will cost you much more to skip school or work. And you now want to live a good successful life. You will make the decision to go to school or work because that will help you move toward your goal of finishing school and living a productive good life.

A good decision-making technique that will always help you make a good decision is . . . think about this book, *Race*.

Results
Accept
Consequences
Engage

This is very simple, let me explain. You are going to flip your normal decision-making process. Usually, we engage in or do something, and then we deal with the consequences, hoping that it will work out okay. Sometimes it does and sometimes it doesn't. But now I want you to start thinking and dealing with the end *results* first. The end results are the outcome of your actions. Before you do anything, no matter what decisions you are faced with, do not do anything. I repeat, "Do not do anything until you think about what kind of results you want at the end of your actions." Then if you are willing to *accept* (agree, approve, receive) the *consequences* (results of one's actions, effects) and if the consequences are good, and if they are going to help you live a successful productive, good, and free life, then, and only then, should you go ahead and *engage* (get involved, enter into, act upon) in your actions. If your actions have any chance of producing negative consequences that will hinder you from living the good life . . . don't do it! Walk away . . . Resist. If the results are positive and you are willing to accept the consequences, then go ahead and engage. If you think about the end results first before you engage in any actions, and you only act when you know that you are going to get positive consequences, you will be making the best decision that you can make. And when you are making a good decision, you will be running at full speed ahead. When you first start using this technique, take the time to write down the consequences, both positive and negative. After a while, it will become second nature and you will not have to write it down, but you will always have to think and go through the process in your mind before you do anything.

You are now running and moving in the right direction. But it appears that your stride is not flowing and moving in the way you would like it to. One thing that will help you for sure to move more smoothly is to pull your pants up and put on a belt. That's right! No more "saggin'." You cannot run very fast or very far with your pants hanging down under your butt. You have to keep grabbing on to them and pulling them up so they want fall off. It is such a waste of time.

How people perceive you is very important. Something as simple as pulling up your pants and standing tall with your head held high and your belt around your waist will make a very big difference in how people perceive you. People will see you as a leader who is serious about life and they will be more willing to help and embrace you on this journey. You must understand that the origin of the word, "saggin'," started in the prison first. Men in the prison wore their pants low as a message and a sign to the other men that they were "available." Saggin' needs to stay in the prison where it started. There is no need for it in our free society. Saggin' is not cool or something new. It is really demoralizing. When you write the word S-A-G-G-I-N backward you get the word N-I-G-G-A-S. Every time you wear your pants down you are demoralizing yourself. You are making a mockery of the black human race. So pull your pants up, be a trendsetter and not a follower. Be one of the first young black men to take a stand and make a change. You can start today. Say this: "saggin' is out" and "looking professional is in." Set the tone and be a leader. You will be surprised at how the simple act of pulling up your pants will gain you much respect from others. This will let people know that you are aspiring to be more than a thug, drug dealer, hustler, or rapper. They will embrace you and do all they can to help you reach your dreams of becoming a CEO, investor, business owner, or whatever you want out of life. Perception is very powerful. Remember that how people perceive you is a reality to them. So give them your best picture. Get your pants up and look like you are serious about changing and running in this race.

Most young Americans are obsessed with wanting material things and wanting to get rich quick. All of your decisions are made trying to get popular designer label clothing, the coolest newest cell phones, iPods, PS2 and 3 games, gold grills, jewelry, money, motorcycles, RIMs, and cars. And there is nothing wrong with wanting things. The problem is that you are not willing to wait and make good decisions that will help you get these things honestly so that you can keep them. You are use to making poor decisions trying to get instant gratification. It is okay to want these things, but you must be willing to wait. You will always make a poor decision, if you are not willing to wait. Never do anything at the spur of the moment without thinking. You've got to be willing to start thinking about the end results of your actions at the beginning before you do anything. Think *race* and only engage if you are willing to accept positive consequences. By doing this, you will be making the best decision that you can make.

This racetrack that you are running on is not straight. In fact, it contains many forks, breaches, and crossroads. Each time you are faced with making a decision you have reached a crossroad. And you must know where you want to go in order to know which path to take. If you don't know where you are going or what you want out of life, then it doesn't matter which path you take. But when you know what you want and you have plans and goals, you need to make sure that you are going in the right direction. Choosing between two paths are often difficult, but not for you because you are now equipped with the *race* decision making technique. Think results first before you do anything, and engage only if you are going to get positive consequences that will be moving you toward your goals.

Chapter Six

Cross the Finish Line

Once you start making good decisions, you will get victory. You now know how to reach the finish line. You must continue to aim at mastering victory in all dimensions of your life. You must look at ways to continue to improve your mind, body, and soul. Your whole existence should be about helping someone else. That is what this race is really all about. You've got to be willing to invest in someone else and help them to get up and get running in this human relay race.

To be effective and on top of your game, you must be willing to read, write, and challenge your mind to increase your mental capacity. Your mind grows stronger when you challenge it. Stimulating your mind by learning new things will make you more alert and responsive. By continually challenging your mind, you will find yourself being able to solve problems and meet life's challenges easier. You are reading this book so you are on the right path of expanding your mind and learning new things. Never think that you know everything. You should always look for ways to grow and improve, no matter how much you think you know. You can always learn something new. When you think that you know it all, and nobody can tell you anything, you are done! You will never advance past where you are at today. You are like a dead man walking. So approach life with the attitude: What can I learn from this situation that will help me to improve and better my life? Take advantage of every opportunity. Let it be a learning process. When you are dealing with life's lessons, make sure that you learn something out of every situation and that you always come out better than when you started.

I know you are young and think that your body is strong and you will live forever. But the truth is, if you keep living, you will get old and die someday. That is why it is so important for you to maximize this process by continuing to improve on taking care of your physical body. After all, you cannot run this race if you are out of shape, overweight, exhausted, or stressed out. You must improve your physical body through proper nutrition, exercise, rest, and stress management. Make sure that you are eating and drinking the right things. Do not abuse you body with cigarettes, drugs, and alcohol. Make sure that you get off the sofa and move around. Do something! Get your body moving. Get at least eight hours of sleep every night and don't let the issues and problems of life stress you out so bad that you give up or check out. After all, you now know how to make good decisions and you are the only one who can take control of your own life and attitude. You only get one body and you must take care of it. Once it is gone, it is gone.

Nothing will help you more to stay focused on this race than developing spiritually (soul). You can do this by reading inspiring literature, meditating, praying, reading the bible, and spending time with nature. This will help you to learn and discover your mission and purpose in life. It will help you to build integrity and spiritual values. You will do the right thing because you want to. It does not matter whether someone is looking at you or not. You will learn to treat other people the way you want to be treated. This is true maturity! This will help you to reinforce your commitment to doing God's will and plan for your life so you can contribute your part to the human relay race as you were created to do.

Last but not least, you must be developing your social and emotional relationships. Make sure that you love and cultivate your family relationships. You must learn to communicate well and be honest and trustworthy in all your relationships. You must respect all authority figures. If you want respect you must give respect. So from this day forward you should never disrespect your parents, teachers, law enforcement, or any other adult in authority. Build new friendships with people who want the same things out of life that you do. Also you must learn to value people who are different from you. When you are willing to work, help, and serve other people as often as possible you have crossed the finish line.

This is a life long journey; so take your time. You should always be looking for ways to improve or better your life no matter how much you have accomplished. Never feel like you have arrived . . . and there is nothing left for you to do. Because as long as you are living, you should always be looking for ways to continue growing in all areas of your life. This is what living the good life is all about. Feeling well and being happy will happen when you are managing all areas of your life properly. I promise you that your life will change and things will get better and better as you continue to improve your mind, body, and soul.

Chapter Seven

You Are a Winner

You are a winner! Hold your head up and act like it. Your future is filled with unlimited potential. You can go anywhere and do anything that your heart desires. You are no longer on the path of poverty, violence, jail, and early death. But instead you have decided to be a winner and do your best at making a difference in your life so that you can live a successful productive good life. You are now empowered with the *race* decision-making process, and you can't be stopped. You are a winner!

Everything that you need to be successful in life is within you. You were born that way. Even if you do not believe in God, if I can get you to believe in this truth you will be successful in life. When you were born in this world you were created with a plan and purpose for your life. I know without a doubt that one of your purposes are to be a willing, successful, participant in this human relay race for life. This includes a good plan for a successful and prosperous life. No matter what negative things people have said about you or did to you, you are a unique individual with gifts, talents, and abilities inside you that you have not even begun to use yet. When you start to use your God-given talents you will fulfill God's purpose that he created you for. You have a job to accomplish in this life that no one can do, but you. This makes you unstoppable. You are not like anyone else; you were not created to be a copycat. You are your own person with your own skills, dreams, talents, and abilities. Be the original that you are. I know it is hard to think that you are this special, because all of your life you were told that you are no good, you were an accident, or something like that. But trust me, you may have been a surprise and a disappointment to your parents, but God had a plan for your life from the very beginning. So run this race with confidence knowing that you are not inferior to anyone. You are equipped with everything that you need. You are not missing or lacking anything to do whatever you want to do in life. You are special and approved by God no matter what has happened or will happen in your life.

Now that you understand that you are somebody special and you deserve to have a good life, you must get a clear vision of what you want to do with your life. What do your success picture look like? Start off by thinking about something that you love doing so much that you would do it for free with every chance you get. What do you want out of this life? What would you do if money or time were not factors? These types of questions and thoughts will help you to decide what direction you need to start moving toward. Start asking yourself a series of questions and be honest and realistic with your answers. What really bothers you? This is the best way to find out about your talents and skills that you possess within you. What would you really like to do? What makes you happy? Think about the things you like doing and what comes easy to you. What are you good at? When you start to answer these questions, you will get an idea on what areas you need to pursue to help you move into your plan and purpose for your life. Think about something that really bothers you. If there is something that really bothers you, you are probably the person who is needed to correct or fix that problem. You must write this information down, so you can review and make sure that you have not missed anything.

Learn to dream big! Don't let anybody kill your dreams. Coach Tony Dungy did not win the Super Bowl in 2007 thinking small. He had to really think above and beyond anything he had ever seen, heard, or done. No black coach had ever coached a team playing in the Super Bowl game, let alone win the Super Bowl. But he believed that he could do it. He acted and worked towards that goal in spite of the odds against him. And he did it! It was not easy, but he continued to work through all his disappointments, rejections, and failures to reach his goal of winning the Super Bowl. And you can reach your goals too. You can do anything that you set your mind too. In June 2008, for the first time in our history we had our first black president nominee (Barack Obama). He had to really think above and beyond anything he had ever seen, heard, or done. But he wasn't afraid to dream and go after what he wanted. And his dream came true on November 4, 2008, when he was elected president of the United States. And the best is yet to come for him, because he is convinced that *"Yes,* we can." And we will with hard work and determination. So dream big! Reach for the unreachable! I like the way Les Brown said it: "Reach for the moon, if you miss the moon you will land among the stars." And that's some good progress.

What are your dreams? You must set some goals. Start with some short-term reachable goals first. Once you have experienced some success in reaching your short-term goals then you can start planning for long-term goals. And you must write your goals down and read and review them often to make sure that you are moving in the right direction. You have to be patient and consistent. You did not get all messed up in just one day, one week, one month, or one year. So it will take you at least that long to get it all together. And believe me, it is worth the wait. Nothing worth having in life is going to be easy. You must be willing to stay focused and do the right things in order to get lasting results. A temporary fix is only good for temporary results. And that is not what we are looking for. We want a lifetime of good results that can be passed on from one generation to the next. You must be convinced that there are no get-rich-quick schemes. I don't care what type of social, economical, or family environment you come from; you can overcome and get what you want out of life, if you are willing to work for it! What separates the winners from the losers are your willingness and attitude to work toward your goals in spite of all the problems and disappointments that will try to discourage and set you back. And, believe me, when you get your goals and mind-set on doing the right thing you will find yourself confused, frustrated, and doubting that things are going to get better and work for you. But this is when you must dig your heels in and be confident that you are doing the right things and you will receive the results you are working towards.

To win in any sport, you have to play by the rules. You have to do the same to win in the relay race for life. If you don't like the game of basketball, football, baseball, tennis, soccer, hockey, or any other sport, you don't have to play. But the human race for life is different. There is no easy way out nor can you refuse to play or participate in life. If you are still breathing and living, you are in the game.

So play or run to the best of your ability. As long as you are giving life your best, you will be successful. The only way to win in this race is to obey the laws of the land, remain free, seek happiness, and be productive. You must have pride, purpose, and respect for yourself. The society needs you to take your place in this amazing human relay race. You are the most valued runner in this race. You are literally needed for the survival of our human race. Don't break the relay race for life. If you don't do your part, nothing that was done before you will matter. Giving up in this race will cost you everything. And that is not an option. You are a winner; believe in yourself, dream big, and keep running towards your dreams with a clear vision in mind. You must keep pressing toward the finish line and help as many people as you can along the way. Helping another person to win is one of the greatest feelings in the world. I haven't met a person yet who does not like to win. You will find out that helping other people is one of the most rewarding parts of your life. That is why I had to write this book so I could help as many people as possible to realize how valuable they are in this human relay race for life. Celebrate yourself because you have finished this book and you are now empowered with all the knowledge you need to have a successful victorious life.

Chapter Eight

Be Encouraged

This is my story: I was born the eighth child in a family of nine children. With my parents, we were a total of eleven members in my immediate family. I was raised in the 1970s and the 1980s. I was blessed to be raised in a two-parent home with lots of love. And I know just having two parents at home is much more than most of you all have today. But I know how challenging it is to be a single parent. I have had to do it by myself for more than eighteen years. I know that most households in today's society are not made up of both the biological parents. I considered my family as poor working class. I love my parents and I know that they did their best. But being a large family with only one income, we didn't have very much. We lived in an old wooden house with no central heating and air-conditioning. In the winter, we slept cold and in the summer we sweated, tossed, and turned all night in the heat. My mother made us keep what we did have clean and in order. She had a gift of stretching food in order to feed all of us. My parents made sure that we had food to eat, clothing to wear, and a place to sleep. We had the basics of what we needed to live. I don't ever remember going hungry, being abused, or neglected. I know! I know! To most of you all this seem like a dream life . . . I know! I know! You were abused, rejected, misused, and neglected. I know your parents were not there for you. I know that they did not provide for you nor take care of you. And some of you can even say that your parents don't even love you; but it is okay. It is all over now and it is in your past. And you cannot do anything to change your past. You are a winner and will be successful anyway in spite of your past. You have already moved on and let all that negative baggage and hurt go.

Regardless of what my parents did or did not do, I wanted much much more out of life. I never had a birthday party as a child, nor have I ever gotten a new bicycle for Christmas. So I quickly learned that material things are not everything, but I did want more out of life. I learned what was important. I know my family loved each other, respected the law, worked hard, and tried their best. This is what I call the true basics of life: values, character, integrity, and morals. This is the foundation of a good life. You must have values, character, integrity, and morals. And if you want to be successful in life, you must have this same foundation. And if you didn't get it as a child, you can learn and create it as an adult. In order to start building your foundation in life, you must start by building *trust*. People must be able to trust you. If people trust you, they know that you are accountable, predictable, dependable, and reliable. Trust is built every day. You must be consistent all the time in your behavior and interactions with others. You must be committed to doing the right things even when you know no one is looking or listening. You will know when others trust you because they will respect you, want to be around you, and they will want to be just like you.

I wanted to be able to give my children more than what I had as a child. I wanted a new house, a car, and a good job so I could have money to enjoy life and take vacations. But how was I going to accomplish this? I did not have a clue, but I did know that I wanted nice things, and I also knew that I was not going to get it by breaking the law and doing illegal things. Because I loved my freedom. I did not want to live my life locked up and caged like an untamed animal. When I turned eighteen years old, I couldn't wait to get away from my parents. After all, they were very strict and things were bad at home. So I went to college out of my home state (what a mistake!). I went to Tuskegee University for all the wrong reasons. College only lasted for a year and I was back home, where I started. I was still not sure what I wanted to do, but I still had the desire to be successful in life. I still wanted a new house, a car, and money. So I knew if I wasn't going to go to school, I had to get a job. So I started working at a "Shop and Go Store" (a self-service gas station). Believe me, I was not going to be able to reach my goal working at gas stations, but it was honest money and I did not have to take a gamble on doing anything illegal that would give me more money but would eventually cost me my freedom. The fast-money game will always be temporary. That type of lifestyle never last long. Eventually, you will get caught and go to jail. So I worked at the Shop and Go Store until something better came along, then I upgraded to a security guard for Ray Willis & Associates Security Company. After working as a security guard for a year, I upgraded to a position of a Juvenile Detention Officer with the State of Florida. In this job I felt confrontable. I understood what was expected of me, and I enjoyed working and dealing with juvenile youthful offenders who were having some problems in obeying the law. Now I was doing something that I really enjoyed, I was pretty good at it; and I was making decent legal money. This was a job that I would have done even if I was not getting paid, but getting paid made me enjoy it better. I had good state benefits, and I was on my way toward my house, car, and money. I was not making enough money to get what I wanted. But I was able to get an apartment and a used car. It was not my ultimate goal, but I was seeing some progress. I was definitely moving in the right direction. I had to reevaluate and make some adjustments to my plans once I became a mother. In life you must be willing to make some changes and try something different when your circumstances change. After my son was born, I knew it was going to take more money for the both of us, plus, I wanted to be able to give and do more for him than my parents had done for me. As a single parent, if I was not willing to make some changes, my son would have been raised just like I was . . . in poverty and lack. So I returned back to school. Keep in mind that all of my actions were moving me toward my goal (house, car, job, money). After many years of working and going to school part-time, I earned my BS degree in education. I received several job promotions and I am currently working as a Juvenile Probation Officer Supervisor with my new house, new car, and job. I'm still looking for the money. After achieving a majority of these goals, I immediately made some new goals. So I am still on my journey on this relay race for life. I still must keep on pressing and running in this race. I cannot give up or be satisfied with where I am. When I think that I have arrived, that is when I will stop growing. So I must keep running and setting new goals. Also I am on a mission to reach out and help as many people as possible. I just wanted to show you that this is not a quick and easy process, but it can be done. Now I am passionate about helping and making a difference in as many peoples' lives as possible. That is why I am writing this book. So stay focused . . . you must understand that this is a life-long race. It will take some time, but you must keep pressing and moving forward. In this race running fast and swift does not mean anything; but if you hold on and endure to the end, you will reach your greatest potential and live the good life.

Remember that you must role-model right positive behavior in front of your children. Your actions speak much louder than anything that you can say. Don't tell them to do as you say and not as you do. Be an example! Be an example! Be an example! Being an example is the most powerful thing that you can do. Also this is the only way to make a difference and shape the next generation. Spend time with your family and form good relationships with respect and open communication. Learn how to talk and share your feelings and concerns. Be home and available to give guidance and supervision to your children. You know that this is what you wanted as a child; so make sure that you do better than what your parents did. This is what real parenting is about. You must be able to lead by example. There is no other way. This is the key to training and raising children. Most children model what they see—good or bad. So make sure that you are being a good role model for your children.

Don't think that you are the only one dealing with problems. We all have some hurdles we must overcome and jump over in this race. In some way all of our families are dysfunctional. Nobody has a perfect problem-free life . . . *nobody*! Remember your race decision-making technique will always help you make a good decision. You must start thinking about the end *results* first before you do anything. No matter what decisions you are faced with, do not do anything until you think about what kind of results you want at the end of your actions. Then and only then if you are willing to *accept* the *consequences* should you go ahead and *engage* in that action or behavior. As long as you don't give up and quit, you will reach your goals. Remember this will not happen overnight. Keep the course, stay focused, and don't quit. No matter what, stay in the *race*. You are a winner and you will get the results that you are looking for. Your best life is yet to come!

Chapter Nine

Running Maintenance

This is a guide for reflective thinking of all the chapters.

Chapter One: Let's Race

1. Do you believe that all races are treated equally and fairly today?
2. What hinders you from being a free law-abiding productive citizen?
3. What are the duties and responsibilities of men concerning their community and family?

Chapter Two: On Your Mark

1. Why is it important to know the history of your race?
2. What does past history have to do with you today?
3. If you refuse to take part in the human relay race for life, what will happen to you, your children, and the next generation?

Chapter Three: Get Ready

1. Explain in detail what you want your life to look like in the next five years?
2. What can you do today to reach your success picture or goal as described in the previous question?
3. Explain what this statement means to you: "Life is 10 percent of what happens to you and 90 percent of how you react."
4. Why is it important to change your negative thinking into positive thinking?

Chapter Four: Go

1. When you take complete responsibility for yourself, you must stop making excuses and blaming others. What are some excuses you have used in the past that you must be willing to let go and get over?
2. What type of parent do you want to be?
3. When you make a mistake or fall down, why is it important to get back up and start over again?

Chapter Five: Run, Run, Run

1. For every action there is a reaction or consequence. How have your previous decisions and choices created the life you have today?
2. If you want to get good successful results or consequences, you must be willing to think before you take any action.

Explain how the *race* decision-making technique can help you do this?

3. Explain what this statement means to you: "You must know where you want to go in order to know which path to take."

Chapter Six: Cross the Finish Line

1. Why is helping others important? And what can you do to help someone else?
2. Feeling well and being happy will occur when you are managing and improving in all areas of your life (mind, body, and soul) how do you plan to accomplish this in each one of these areas?
3. In order to develop good relationships and true maturity, you must treat others the way you want to be treated. Why should you give respect even if you are being disrespected?

Chapter Seven: You Are a Winner

1. What makes you happy?
2. If you could do anything you wanted with no regard to money, time, or importance. What would you do?
3. What comes easy to you? What do you do well?
4. What bothers you more than anything in this world?

Chapter Eight: Be Encouraged

1. Values, character, integrity, and morals are needed to form a basic foundation for life. Look up each word in the dictionary and write down their definitions. Then think of ways you can use this information to show others that you have a good foundation?

2. You must start by building trust with everyone you come in contact with. Why must you be trustworthy?

3. Explain what a role model is? And what leading by example means?

Chapter Nine: Running Maintenance
Race Decision-making Technique

Results Accept Consequences Engage

What is the decision you must make?
Decision _____

_____
_____
_____
_____
_____
_____

Think about the end results first—both good (positive) and bad (negative).

#1. *Results*—**End product—Outcome—Consequences**

Positive/Good Results	*Negative/Bad Results*
_____	_____
_____	_____
_____	_____
_____	_____
_____	_____
_____	_____
_____	_____
_____	_____

#2. *Accept.* **Pick the list from above that will help you get positive results/*consequences*. Then *engage*, get involved, and enter into action.**